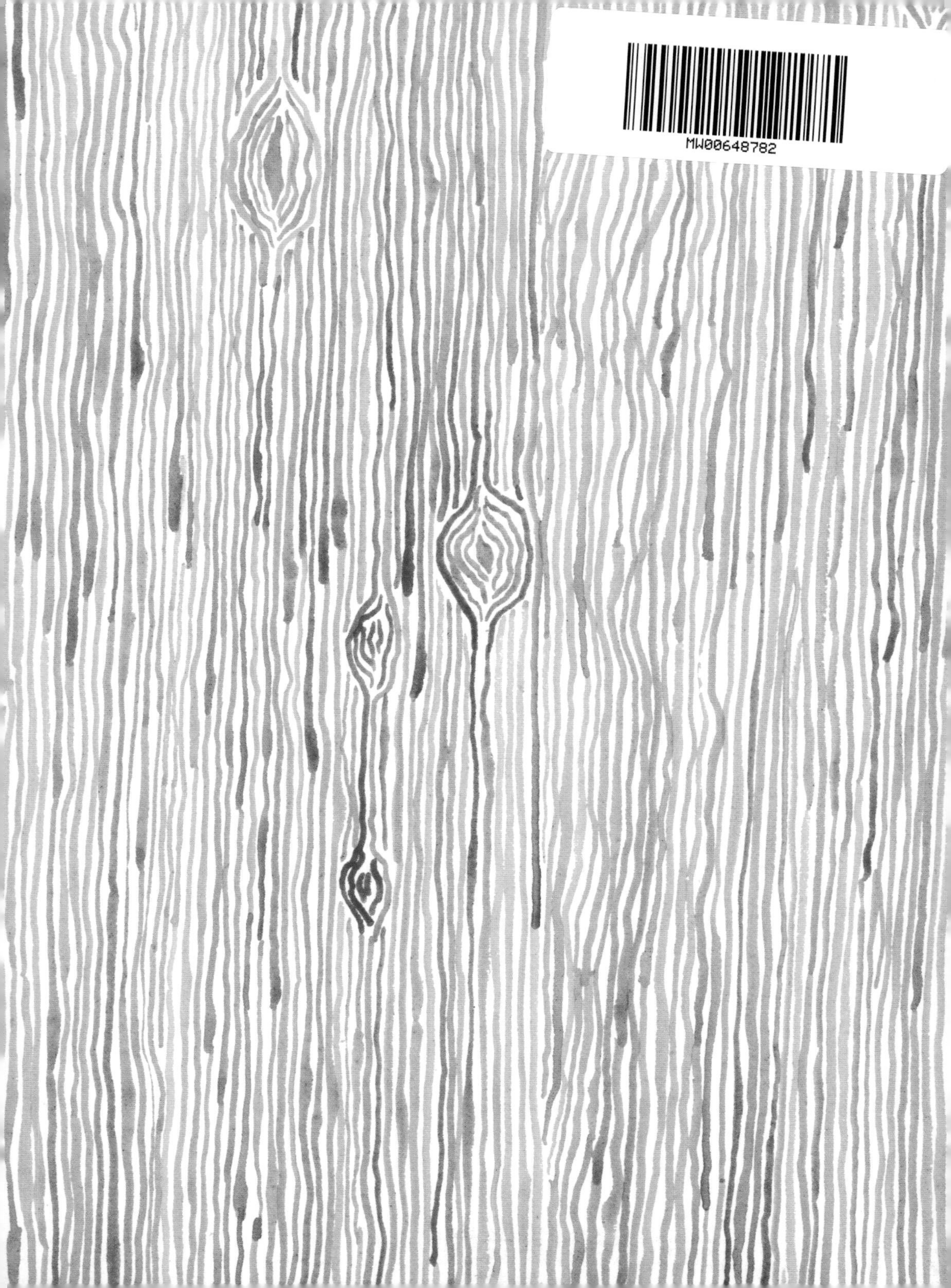

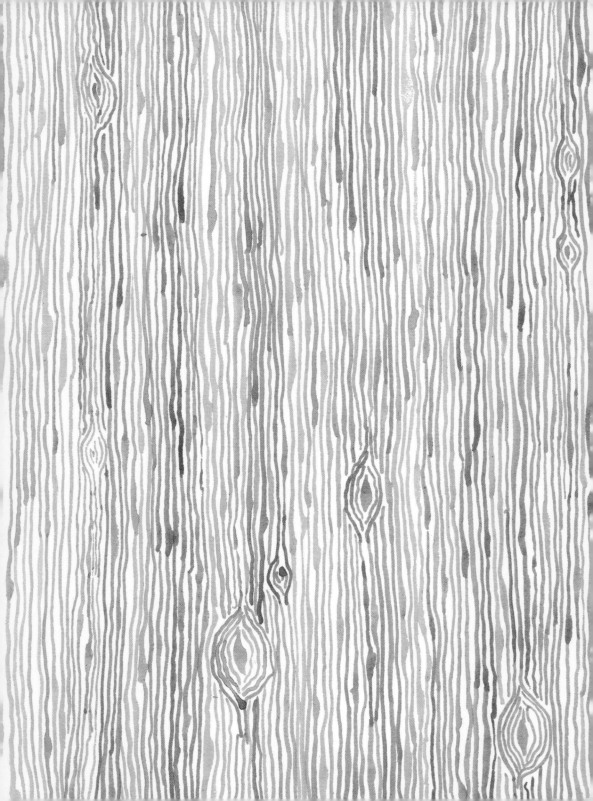

More
than a
Little

Written by: M.H. Clark
Illustrated by: Cécile Metzger

I more than a little appreciate you,
and the person you are, and the things that you do.

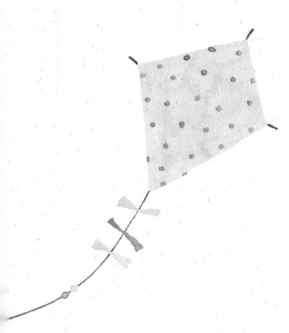

You more than a little bit matter to me.
Where you are, things are brighter. It's easy to see.

You're a gem, you're a peach, you're a wonderful friend,
but there's more to the story than that, even then...

You're gooder than good, and you're kinder than kind.
I need better words than I'm able to find.

There isn't a giant enough dictionary
to name all the brilliance and goodness you carry.

There isn't an obvious way to describe
all the light and the spirit you carry inside.

I could say things like *generous*, *bighearted*, and *dear*.
I could tell you I'm endlessly glad you are here.

I could say that just knowing you're part of my life
makes even the rainy days feel more alright.

There's a magic that's yours, and it's like nothing else.
It's something you share just by being yourself.

It's hard to define, but I know that it's real.
It's something my head and my heart simply feel.

The one thing that all of the brightest days share?
I can look back and see that it's you:
you were there.

So I'm saying all this in the hopes that you'll know
what a difference you make everywhere that you go.

And that when I list out the best things in my life,

I write your name down.

(Not just once, you know. Twice.)

So I guess that I'm writing this all just to say
that if I could share some of what you've sent my way...

Then reading this makes you feel sparkling straight through,
because *that* is exactly what *you* always do.

Yes, this is a thank you, for all that you are.
The good that you do in this world travels far.

And even though all the right words don't exist,
I wanted to write down and share all of this...

I more than a little appreciate you.
It's more like a whole heaping lot.
(This is true.)

To get it just right,
I would need a whole book.
Come to think of it,
well, that is just what it took.

COMPENDIUM®
live inspired

Written by: M.H. Clark
Illustrated by: Cécile Metzger
Edited by: Cindy Wetterlund
Art Directed by: Chelsea Bianchini

ISBN: 978-1-970147-44-5

2nd printing. Printed in China with soy inks on FSC®-Mix certified paper.

Create meaningful moments with gifts that inspire.

CONNECT WITH US
live-inspired.com | sayhello@compendiuminc.com

    @compendiumliveinspired
#compendiumliveinspired

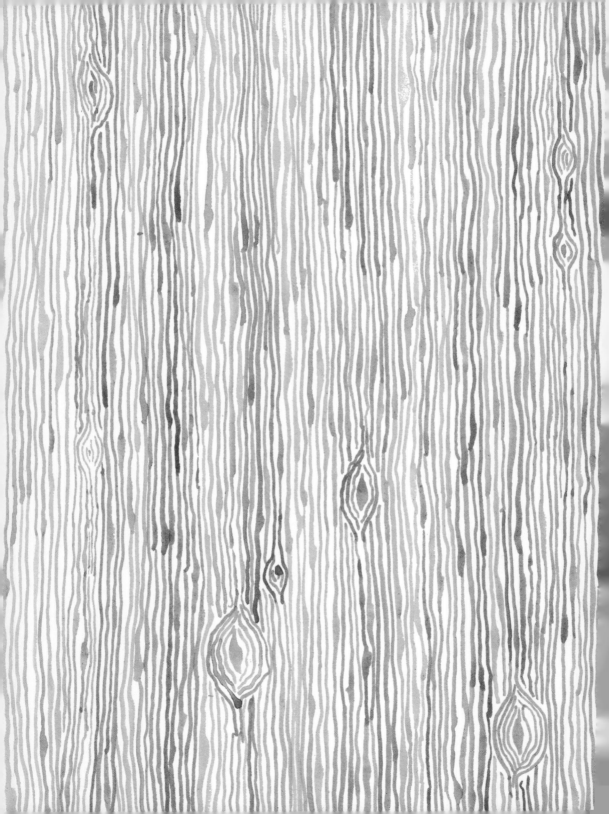